How to Draw
Dinosaurs

This book is dedicated to Jordan.

Published in the United States of America by The Child's World®
PO Box 326 • Chanhassen, MN 55317-0326
800-599-READ • www.childsworld.com

Acknowledgments
Design and Production: The Creative Spark, San Juan Capistrano, CA
Series Editor: Elizabeth Sirimarco Budd
Illustration: Rob Court

Library of Congress Cataloging-in-Publication Data
Court, Robert, 1956–
  How to draw dinosaurs / by Rob Court.
     p. cm. — (The Scribbles Institute)
  ISBN 1-59296-150-9 (library bound : alk. paper)
 1. Dinosaurs in art—Juvenile literature. 2. Drawing—Technique—Juvenile
literature. I. Title.
 NC780.5.C68 2004
 743.6—dc22

                              2004003732

How to Draw
Dinosaurs

Rob Court

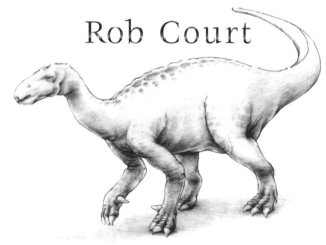

It is not enough to believe what you see,
you must also understand what you see.

—Leonardo da Vinci

Parents and Teachers,

Children love to draw! It is an essential part of a child's learning process. Drawing skills are used to investigate both natural and constructed environments, record observations, solve problems, and express ideas. The purpose of this book is to help students advance through the challenges of drawing and to encourage the use of drawing in school projects. The reader is also introduced to the elements of visual art—lines, shapes, patterns, form, texture, light, space, and color—and their importance in the fundamentals of drawing.

The Scribbles Institute is devoted to educational materials that keep creativity in our schools and in our children's dreams. Our mission is to empower young creative thinkers with knowledge in visual art while helping to improve their drawing skills. Students, parents, and teachers are invited to visit our Web site—www.scribblesinstitute.com—for useful information and guidance. You can even get advice from a drawing coach!

Contents

Dinosaurs Are Exciting to Draw!   6

Drawing with Shapes   8

Drawing with Lines   9

Three-Dimensional Form   14

Light and Shadows   16

Patterns   18

Texture   20

Space and Composition   24

Drawing with Color   28

The Artist's Studio   31

Glossary   32

Index   32

Dinosaurs Are Exciting to Draw!

You can draw a terrifying dinosaur with sharp teeth and dangerous claws. Or you can draw a funny little creature scurrying through the jungle, stealing eggs or eating insects.

The easy steps in this book will help you draw dinosaurs for school projects or for fun. Find a big piece of paper and a pencil. You can get started right now!

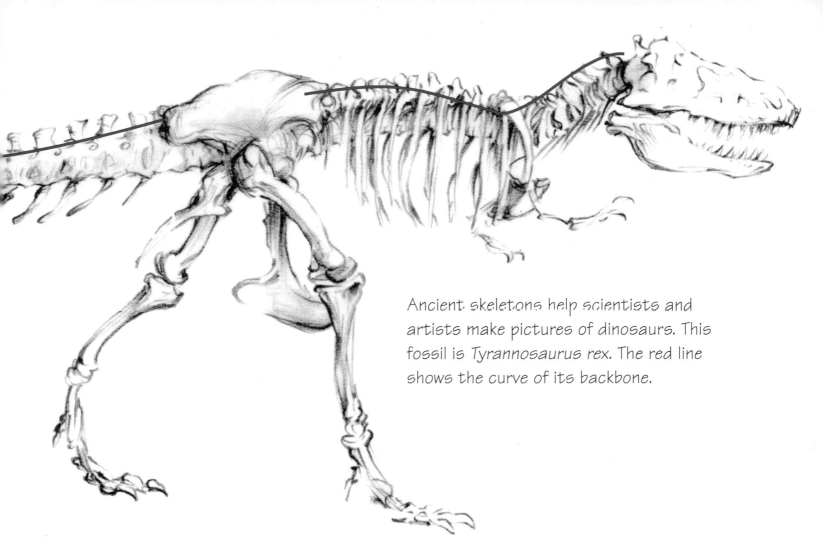

Ancient skeletons help scientists and artists make pictures of dinosaurs. This fossil is *Tyrannosaurus rex*. The red line shows the curve of its backbone.

Dinosaur means "terrible lizard." These creatures lived millions of years ago. They are not alive today, so artists can only imagine what they looked like. Some dinosaurs were very large. They moved slowly but took huge steps. Others were as small as a chicken and could move quite fast. Let's learn to draw *Tyrannosaurus rex*, also known as *T. rex.*

T. rex was large and active. It was a ferocious meat eater with sharp teeth and claws for hunting. As you draw, imagine how its strong bones supported its powerful muscles.

Drawing with Shapes

Drawing a dinosaur is easy when you start with basic shapes. Shapes like circles and ovals show the position of its head and body. Sketch these shapes lightly. That way, you can erase them later as you finish your picture.

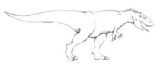

Tyrannosaurus
Length: 33–46 feet
(10–14 meters)
Weight: 4–6 tons
(3.5–5.5 metric tons)
Meat eater

1 Sketch a large circle and oval for the body of T. rex. Another oval is the basic shape of its head and powerful jaw. Sketch a curved line for the backbone, neck, and tail.

A long, curved line connects the shapes of T. rex's body.

2 Ovals show the position of the leg and arm muscles. Also sketch shapes for the neck and tail. Next, sketch shapes for the small front claws and deadly hind claws. A small oval marks the position of the eye.

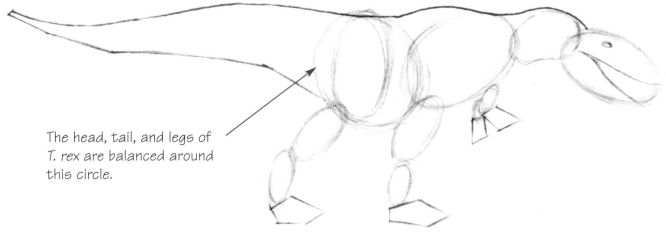

The head, tail, and legs of T. rex are balanced around this circle.

Drawing with Lines

Now draw an **outline** around the edge of the shapes you've made. This will form the dinosaur's body. Keep drawing until you like the outline. Remember to draw lightly. Then you can erase if you need to.

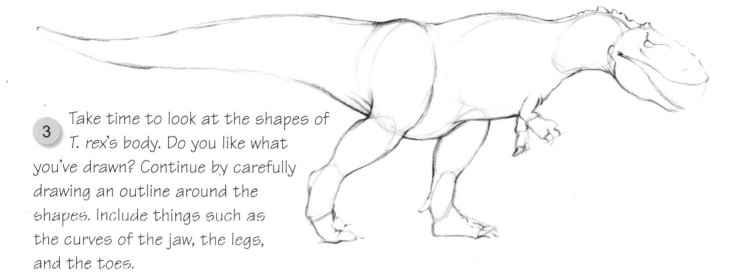

3 Take time to look at the shapes of T. rex's body. Do you like what you've drawn? Continue by carefully drawing an outline around the shapes. Include things such as the curves of the jaw, the legs, and the toes.

4 Using angled and curved lines, carefully draw a darker outline to finish your picture (see page 27 to learn more about pencils). Remember, T. rex was a meat eater. Don't forget to **illustrate** details like the teeth and claws. Use both straight and curved lines.

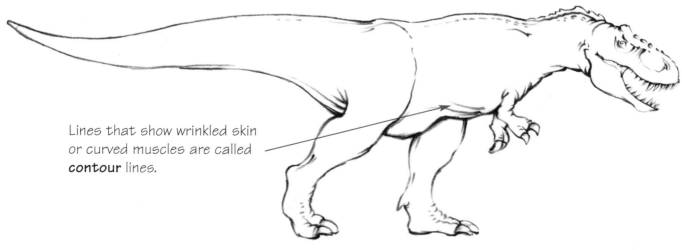

Lines that show wrinkled skin or curved muscles are called **contour** lines.

9

You can draw many kinds of dinosaurs with shapes and lines.

1 Sketch two ovals for the huge body of *Diplodocus*. Its head was much smaller than its body. A curved line makes its neck, backbone, and long, slender tail.

Diplodocus
Length: Up to 90 feet
(27.5 meters)
Weight: Up to 20 tons
(18 metric tons)
Plant eater

2 Draw ovals for its legs. Lightly sketch the area for a long neck and long, powerful tail. Imagine how a whip moves when drawing the tail. *Diplodocus* probably used its tail against predators.

Diplodocus means "two beam." Notice how its legs support and balance its heavy body.

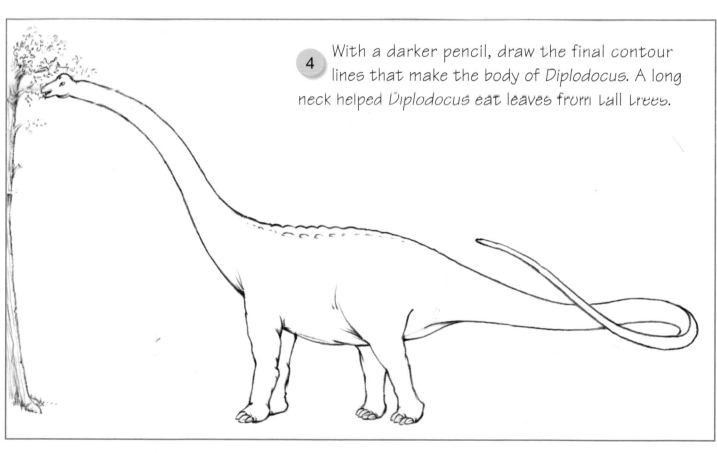

3 Do you like the shapes you've drawn for *Diplodocus*? Keep sketching until you like them. Next, carefully draw a darker outline for its body.

Erase lines to show this part of the tail overlapping, or in front of, the rest of it.

4 With a darker pencil, draw the final contour lines that make the body of *Diplodocus*. A long neck helped *Diplodocus* eat leaves from tall trees.

Draw Big! Use the whole sheet of paper to draw this plant-eating giant.

Triceratops

Length: 30 feet
(9 meters)
Weight: Up to 6 tons
(5.5 metric tons)
Plant eater

1 Sketch a large oval for the body of *Triceratops*. Two more ovals show where you will draw its strong legs. Now draw the shape that shows the position of its head. Add a curved line for the backbone and tail.

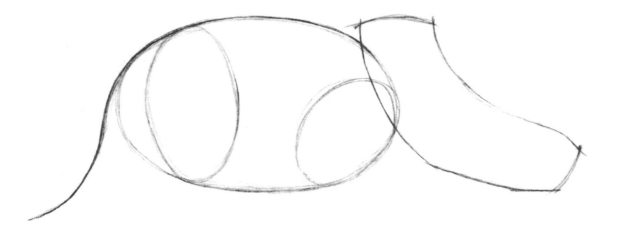

2 *Triceratops* means "three-horned face." Lightly sketch shapes for the sharp horns on the head of *Triceratops*. Draw ovals for its legs. Add the shapes for its feet and tail. A small oval shows the eye's position.

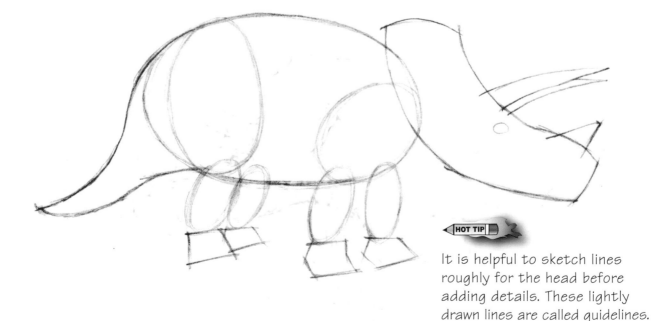

HOT TIP

It is helpful to sketch lines roughly for the head before adding details. These lightly drawn lines are called guidelines.

3 Now draw the outline of *Triceratops*. Take time to include details. Notice the bony edge around the top of its head and the long, pointy snout. Did you draw the horns so they look hard and pointed?

4 *Triceratops* has distinct features that need careful attention. Notice the pattern of pointed, bony spikes that surround its skull. Carefully draw the final contour lines for the rough skin and bony features of *Triceratops*.

Contour lines show where skin surrounds the horn.

Three-Dimensional Form

Now comes the best part! It's time to make the dinosaur look real. With practice, you can change flat shapes into three-dimensional or "3-D" forms.

side view

three-quarter view

Drawing a Three-Quarter View of *Triceratops*

Imagine this dinosaur slowly turning its body so that its giant horns almost point toward you. This is a three-quarter view of *Triceratops*. The shapes are different from the side view shown on pages 12 and 13.

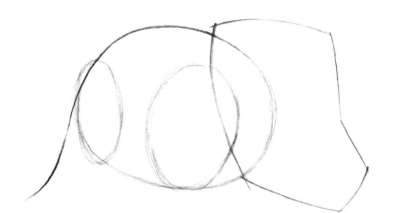

1 Start sketching a large oval for its body. Two smaller ovals set the position for its hind and front legs. Now draw the shape for its massive head. Remember to draw lightly so you can erase if you want to.

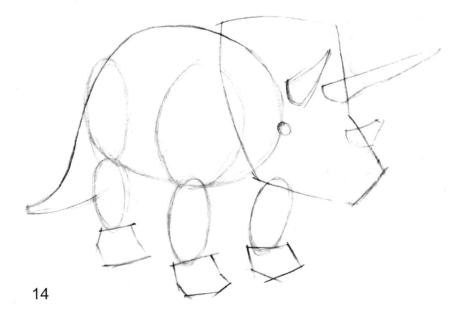

2 Sketch the shapes for the bulky legs. Lightly sketch the shape of its head, horns, and tail. You're beginning to see the 3-D form of this prehistoric giant! Add an oval for the eye.

3 Continue sketching lines until you begin to see the contours, or curves, of its body, legs, and tail. This is called tightening the lines of your drawing. Imagine how the tough, leathery skin covers different muscles.

4 You've drawn the rough outlines that form *Triceratops*. Now draw its darker, final outlines. Draw curved lines that show the 3-D contours of its body, not just flat shapes.

An Egg Doesn't Always Look Egg-Shaped

The form of a dinosaur egg changes when you see it from different angles.

side view

three-quarter view

front view

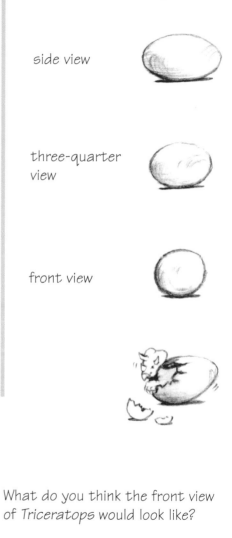

What do you think the front view of *Triceratops* would look like?

15

Light and Shadows

Shadows help you see the ground and the dinosaur's form.

Iguanodon

Length: Up to 30 feet
(9 meters)
Weight: 4–5 tons
(3.5–4.5 metric tons)
Plant eater

1 Start with basic oval shapes to begin drawing *Iguanodon*. Remember to connect these shapes with a line that makes the curve of its spine.

A kidney shape shows the position of the dinosaur's long neck.

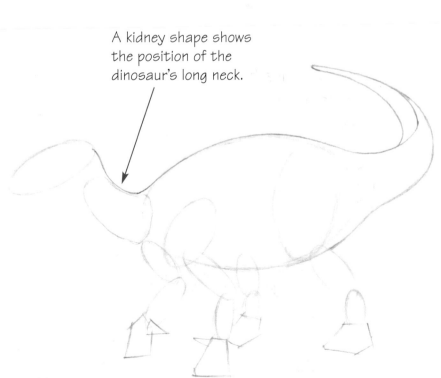

2 *Iguanodon* walked on all four legs but could stand upright to eat leaves. Sketch ovals for legs and add shapes for its feet. Notice the sharp, bony spikes near its front toes. Sketch curved lines for the tail.

 HOT TIP

Press lightly with your pencil when drawing the guidelines that make these basic shapes. This makes it easier to erase the shapes before drawing the shadows shown in step 4.

3 Before adding shadows, carefully draw outlines that form the body of *Iguanodon*.

Light Source

A place where light comes from is called a light source. The sun is a light source. A lamp is also a light source. In the drawing below, a light source shines on a sphere. How do the shadows change as the light changes position?

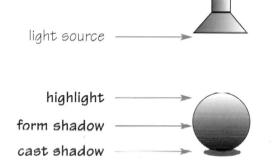

light source

highlight
form shadow
cast shadow

4 Start drawing shadows in areas where no light shines from the light source. Hold your pencil on its side, press firmly, and begin drawing the darkest shadows on *Iguanodon*'s body. Shadows will be lighter where more light from the light source is visible. Lighten the pressure on your pencil as you draw lighter shadows. Fade the shadows away to the white of the paper where there are high-lights. Remember to draw the cast shadow on the ground beneath *Iguanodon*'s feet.

cast shadow

17

Patterns

It's fun to imagine the patterns on a dinosaur's skin. By repeating lines or shapes, you can draw patterns. Living relatives of dinosaurs, such as turtles, lizards, and crocodiles, can give you ideas to create patterns.

Elasmosaurus
Length: 46 feet
(14 meters)
Weight: 2.5 tons
(2.25 metric tons)
Fish eater

1 This huge marine reptile used its long neck to catch fish. Start by drawing a long and narrow oval for its body. Next draw a small oval for its head. A long, curved line makes the spine of *Elasmosaurus*.

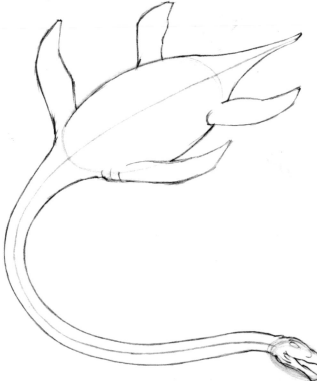

2 *Elasmosaurus* lived in the ocean, so it had flippers instead of legs. Draw the basic shapes where its flippers will be. Lightly draw the curved guidelines for the neck and tail.

3 Carefully draw the outlines that make the outer edges of the body. Now draw the curved outlines of its neck. Sometimes artists make several sketches before the smooth, curved lines look just right.

4 Finish drawing the form of this dinosaur's huge body by adding darker contour lines. Now have fun making lines and shapes to create the pattern of the dinosaur's skin.

Pattern Ideas

Texture

How the surface of something feels is called texture. The texture of dinosaur skin was very rough and bumpy. You can draw lines and patterns to create different textures.

Ankylosaurus

Length: 33–36 feet
(10–11 meters)
Weight: 4 tons
(3.5 metric tons)
Plant eater

1 Start by drawing a large oval for Ankylosaurus' body. A smaller oval makes the bony club at the end of its tail. Next, draw the shape for its head. Connect the shapes with a curved line that makes the backbone and tail of Ankylosaurus.

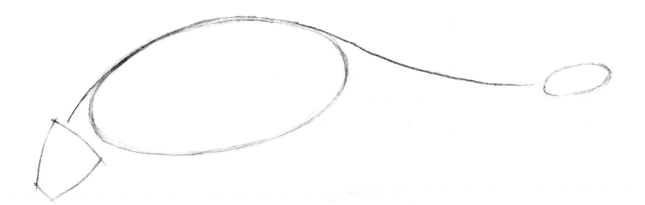

2 Ankylosaurus had bony armor plates and horns to protect it from large meat eaters. Draw the shapes for the strong legs that hold its compact body. Add the rows of triangle shapes that will be its bony armor.

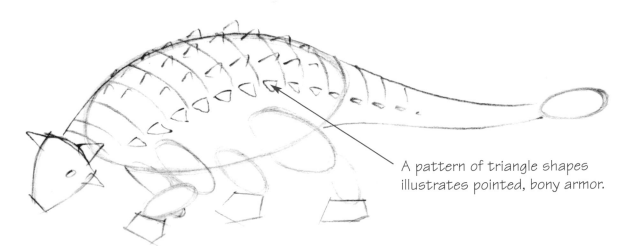

A pattern of triangle shapes illustrates pointed, bony armor.

3 Sketch the outlines that form the body of Ankylosaurus. Remember to keep sketching light lines until you like what you've drawn. Lightly draw the lines that make the bony plates of armor.

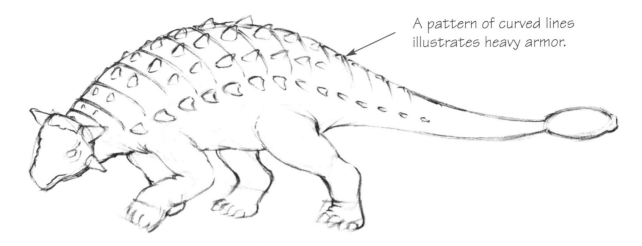

A pattern of curved lines illustrates heavy armor.

4 It's time to add details. Ankylosaurus' skin probably had a thick, scaly pattern. Draw a pattern for its armor. The texture of its pointed, bony horns was smoother than its skin of armor. Draw straight and curved lines to show the difference in texture.

Drawing scales only in a small area suggests that this bony armor covered all of Ankylosaurus. Unlike overlapping scales found on fish, scales on dinosaur skins were connected like tiles on a floor.

Flying reptiles lived during the time of dinosaurs. The texture of their bodies was furry. They had wings of leathery skin.

Pterodactylus

Length: Wingspan up to 2 feet
(120 centimeters)
Weight: Up to 3 pounds
(1.3 kilograms)
Fish eater

1 The body of *Pterodactylus* was shorter than its head and beak. First draw an oval for its body. Next draw the shape of its head and long beak. A curved line creates its spine and short tail. Notice the short, curved line that makes its neck.

2 *Pterodactylus* had wings. Use angled lines to show their shape. Next draw the shapes for its legs and claws. Notice the position of the claws on the wings. A tiny oval shows the position of its eye. For the mouth, draw a line that's nearly straight. *Pterodactylus* used its long beak to scoop up fish from the ocean.

The shape of *Pterodactylus'* wings are similar to those of an airplane.

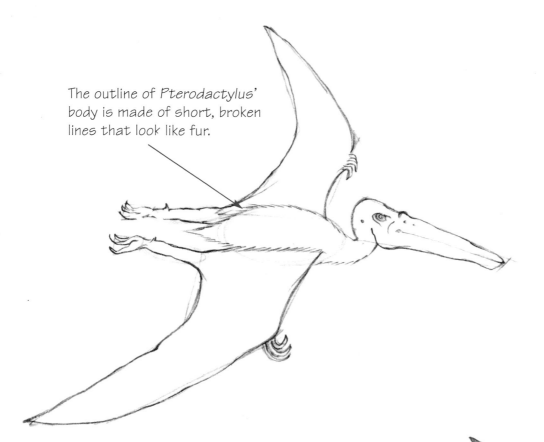

The outline of *Pterodactylus'* body is made of short, broken lines that look like fur.

3 Begin drawing the outline of the wings and body. Notice the slight curve of its leathery wings. Start sketching the outlines that show the fur and the curves of its hard beak.

4 Begin drawing the final contour lines that form the body of *Pterodactylus*. First, draw the short lines that create the texture of its fur. Next, make the contour lines that show the texture of stretched skin for its wings. Use a strong outline for its long, hard beak. Be sure to add details such as its pointed teeth, the breathing holes in its beak, and its sharp claws.

Space and Composition

The white space on your paper can be transformed into an environment where dinosaurs live. The way you divide and arrange the space is a drawing's composition. Begin your composition by drawing the **horizon line.** This shows where the ground meets the sky. Draw it to the edges of your paper. Next begin adding the shapes for *Stegosaurus*.

Stegosaurus

Length: Up to 30 feet
(9 meters)
Weight: Up to 2 tons
(1.8 metric tons)
Plant eater

1 Draw a large oval for the shape of *Stegosaurus'* body. A small oval shows its head. A curved line makes the arch of its back and tail.

horizon line

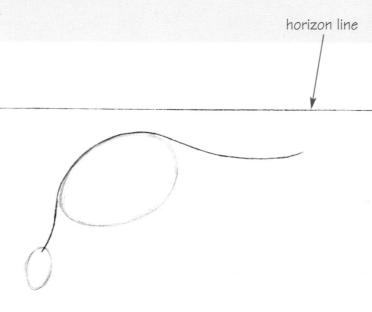

2 Smaller ovals form its back and front legs. Sketch the shapes for the feet and neck area. Now draw angled lines for the shape of the large plates. You can repeat the same shape, making each one smaller moving out from the middle toward its head and the tip of its tail.

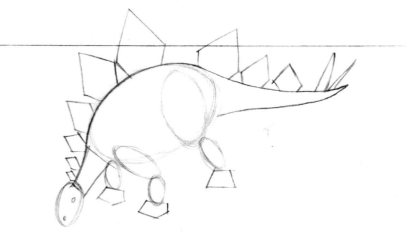

24

Erase the parts of the horizon line that you wouldn't be able to see because they are behind Stegosaurus.

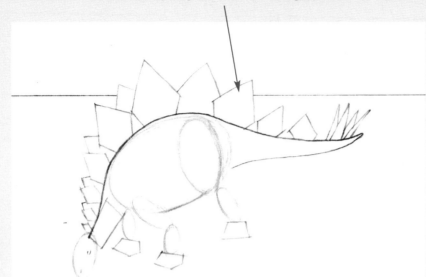

3 Draw more bony plates to fill the space behind the plates you've already drawn. Also draw spikes on the end of the tail of Stegosaurus. You can start to see the space where Stegosaurus is standing. This space is called the **foreground.**

Artists spend time planning the composition of their artwork. Animation artists plan how scenes will look in movies and cartoons. Book illustrators think about how drawings will fit with text on a page.

Overlapping makes the small rock look as if it is in front of the bigger one.

4 Now you can sketch other areas of your composition. The space behind Stegosaurus is called the **background.** Sketch the palm trees in the background. The tree that is farther away is smaller. Draw mountains in the distance, on the horizon line.

5 Begin drawing darker contour lines that form the body of *Stegosaurus* and the other parts of your composition. Notice how the palm trees overlap the mountains in the background. Are they closer or farther away than the mountains?

6 Draw lines on the bony plates to illustrate their texture. Add a pattern of bony bumps on the dinosaur's back and other details on its body. To complete your drawing, carefully add form and cast shadows to *Stegosaurus'* body and to the ground.

Shade the palm tree to give it a gray tone.

Which Pencil Should You Use?

A standard "2B" or "2SOFT"' pencil works well for most drawings, but other pencils can make your drawing even more interesting.

Pencils are numbered according to how hard or soft the lead is. You'll find this number written on the pencil. A number combined with the letter "H" means the lead is hard (2H, 3H, 4H, etc.). When you draw with hard leads, the larger the number you use, the lighter and thinner your lines will be.

A number combined with the letter "B" means the lead is soft (2B, 4B, 6B, etc.). The lines you draw will get darker and thicker with larger numbers. Sometimes you will read "2SOFT" or "2B" on standard pencils used for schoolwork. When you see the letter "F" on a pencil, it means the pencil is of medium hardness.

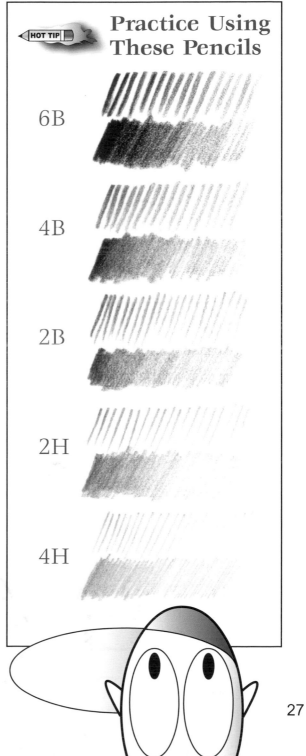

HOT TIP

Practice Using These Pencils

6B

4B

2B

2H

4H

Drawing with Color

Colors and patterns of dinosaurs' skin probably helped them to hide in their surroundings. Dinosaurs that lived in the forest may have been blue, green, and yellow. Those that lived in the desert may have been brown, gray, and red. Which colors would you choose for a dinosaur that lived in the sea? By using colored pencils, you can make your picture more exciting.

Velociraptor
Length: Up to 6 feet
(2 meters)
Weight: Up to 33 pounds
(15 kilograms)
Meat eater

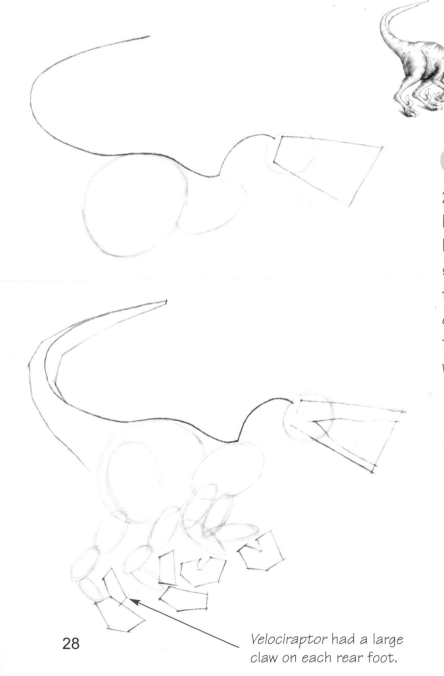

1 Begin by drawing shapes and guidelines with a standard number 2 pencil. A large and small oval form its body. Draw a circle for the dinosaur's head. Using straight lines, make the shape for its powerful jaw. A curved line for its backbone and tail connects the different shapes of its body. Remember to draw light guidelines so that they will be easy to erase.

2 *Velociraptor* was not much taller than a man. It was a swift and ferocious hunter. While adding ovals for the front and rear legs, imagine the muscles that helped this dinosaur chase its prey. Add the guidelines for its tail, its front claws, and its rear claws. Also include lines for the placement of its mouth.

Velociraptor had a large claw on each rear foot.

3 Take time to create the contour lines that form the body of *Velociraptor*. Begin adding details such as its tongue and powerful claws. When you like the lines you've drawn, carefully erase all guidelines and prepare to add color.

Primary Colors

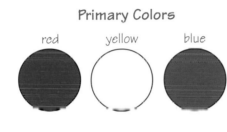

red   yellow   blue

Secondary Colors

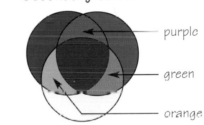

purple

green

orange

 HOT TIP

Mixing primary colors creates secondary colors.

Adding one color on top of another is called layering. To learn how to layer primary colors, try using only yellow, blue, and red, along with black, in this drawing.

4 Start by lightly shading *Velociraptor*'s entire body with a yellow pencil. Think about the direction from where the light source is shining. Apply more pressure to darken areas where there are shadows.

5 Now add a layer of blue. Notice how a pattern is created in areas where blue is blended with yellow. Notice the pattern of yellow and green.

Mixing Colored Pencils is Fun!

red

blue

yellow

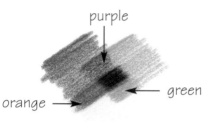

purple

orange →

← green

6 Fun things start to happen when you add the color red to *Velociraptor's* skin. What happens when red blends with yellow and blue?

Light red makes the pinkish color for its tongue and mouth. Next, use your black pencil to blend areas where there are shadows. Remember to make darker shadows that are farther away from the light source. Shading with black creates the 3-D form of *Velociraptor*.

Highlights and shadows create realistic details.

The Artist's Studio

Artists need a special place where they can relax and concentrate on their work.

Computer
For school art projects, a computer is a great source of visual ideas and information. Learning to use drawing and animation software is fun, too.

Easel
Typically made of wood, an easel securely holds the canvas or board on which you are painting.

Light
When making artwork in your studio, you will need a powerful light source.

Music
Drawing is more fun while listening to your favorite tracks!

Tools
Drawing pencils, pens, paintbrushes, scissors, rulers, and triangles (for drawing angled lines) should be kept in one place so that you can grab them quickly. To keep a sharp point on your pencil, have a sharpener nearby.

Light table
This device can help you trace pictures.

Library
Books of all kinds are a great way to find ideas and inspiration.

Portfolio
This carrying case protects your artwork and drawing tablets.

Drawing table
You need a large, clean tabletop on which to draw.

Chair
A comfortable chair is important when you spend a lot of time drawing.

Storage
Use drawers and bins to store paint, colored pencils, pastels, and other supplies.

Glossary

Background is the area toward the back of a picture, behind other things.

A **cast shadow** is the shadow that a person, animal, or object throws on the ground, a wall, or other feature.

A **contour** is the outline of something; in your drawings, a contour line follows the natural shape of the dinosaurs.

Foreground is the area toward the front of a picture, in front of other things.

A **form shadow** is a shadow in a drawing that shows the form or shape of a person, animal, or object.

A **highlight** is the area (or areas) in a drawing that receives the most light from the light source.

The **horizon line** is the point in a drawing where the sky and earth appear to meet.

To **illustrate** is to show or explain something through drawings, words, or stories.

An **outline** is a line that shows the shape of an object, animal, or person.

Index

background, 25, 26
color, 28–30
composition, 24–26
contour, 9, 11, 13, 15, 19, 23, 26, 29
foreground, 25
guideline, 12, 16, 18, 28, 29
highlight, 17, 30
light source, 17, 29, 30, 31
line, 9, 10
outline, 9, 11, 13, 15, 17, 19, 21, 23
pattern, 13, 18–19, 20, 21, 26, 30
pencils, selecting, 27
shadow, 16–17, 26, 29, 30
shape, 8, 10
studio, artist's, 31
texture, 20–23
three-dimensional (3D) form, 14–15, 30

About the Author

Rob Court is a designer and illustrator. He started the Scribbles Institute™ to help people learn about the importance of drawing and visual art.